Bags of FOLK
for violin

Arranged by
Mary Cohen

© 2008 by Faber Music Ltd
This edition first published in 2008
3 Queen Square London WC1N 3AU
Music processed by Jeanne Roberts
Cover designed by Susan Clarke
Illustration by Andy Cooke
Printed in England by Caligraving Ltd
All rights reserved

ISBN10: 0-571-53114-8
EAN13: 978-0-571-53114-1

To buy Faber Music publications or to find out about the full range of titles available
please contact your local music retailer or Faber Music sales enquiries:

Faber Music Ltd, Burnt Mill, Elizabeth Way, Harlow CM20 2HX
Tel: +44 (0) 1279 82 89 82   Fax: +44 (0) 1279 82 89 83
sales@fabermusic.com   fabermusic.com

Foreword

Bags of Folk is an introduction to the wonderful world of traditional music, and contains a mixture of airs and dances — great tunes from England, Scotland, Ireland, Wales and the USA. The music has been carefully selected so that it is great to play without needing any accompaniment, although you might like to form a fiddle band with your friends!

Folk music is always changing and developing, and there are lots of ways to personalise tunes, once you have mastered the notes. For instance, try adding extra 'slides' and 'grace' notes, or playing some of the hornpipes (marked with an * below) in 'swung' rhythm, so that ♫ becomes ♩♪. More advanced players will particularly enjoy revisiting this book and developing tunes in this way.

Contents

John Ryan's polka

Traditional Irish

Goddesses

Traditional English

All through the night

Traditional Welsh

4

G Major.

Shaker melody

Traditional American

D Major -

Helston furry dance

Traditional English

The blue bell of Scotland

Traditional Scottish

Early one morning

Telling a story . . .

Traditional English

The fox and the grapes

Cheerfully No more than ♩132

By Memory 13-5

Traditional Welsh

Nonesuch

Very rhythmically

Traditional English

6

Star of the County Down

Traditional Irish

Argeers

Traditional English

Dargason

Traditional English

The waters of Tyne

Traditional English

The dashing white sergeant

Traditional Scottish

The wind that shakes the barley

Traditional Irish

Soldier's joy

Traditional English

The Rakes of Mallow

Good humoured

Traditional Irish

She moved through the fair

Wistfully

Traditional Irish

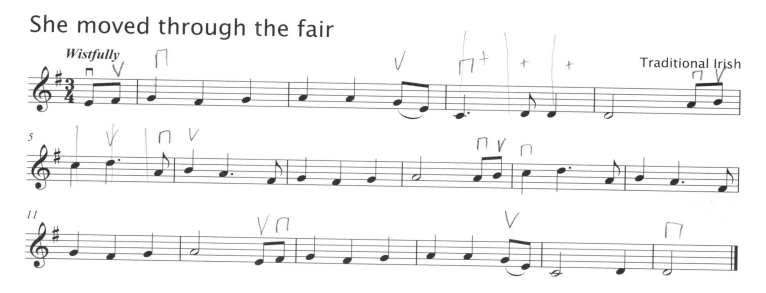

Jenny pluck pears

With a crisp rhythm

Traditional English

The water is wide

Traditional English

Roaring jelly

Traditional English

20 – 7

Down by the Salley Gardens

Smoothly

Traditional Irish

Harvest home

Lively

Traditional English

Circassian circle

Twisting and turning!

Traditional English

Lannigan's ball

Dancing

Traditional Irish

The trumpet hornpipe

Rolling along

Traditional English

The lark in the clear air

With singing tone

Traditional Irish

Staten Island

Traditional Irish

Lively

Grimstock

Traditional English

Skipping

The girl I left behind me

Traditional English

Boastfully

Rufty tufty

Very rhythmically

Traditional English

Sailor's hornpipe

Steady as she goes!

Traditional English

Chestnut

Traditional English

Vigorously

The flop-eared mule

Traditional American

Persevering...